Suing A Global Corporation

Suing A Global Corporation

WHAT TO DO AND NOT DO IN YOUR PURSUIT FOR JUSTICE

ANN P.B

Library of Congress Control Number: 2011961260
ISBN: Hardcover   978-1-4653-8573-4
                   Softcover   978-1-4653-8572-7
                   Ebook   978-1-4653-8574-1

This book was printed in the United States of America.

To order additional copies of this book, contact:
Xlibris Corporation
1-888-795-4274
www.Xlibris.com
Orders@Xlibris.com
103764

CONTENTS

To all of you employees that have been dedicated to a company and found yourself in a situation where you have been or now being targeted for unfair treatment.

This treatment can come in the form of racism, harassment, wrongful termination, and/or retaliation. These events can cause stress, physical illness, and anger to the point of revenge. I hope what I am about to share will alert you of what to do and not do during the ordeals and struggles that you may have faced or are facing right now.

Good luck in pursuing justice!

ABOUT THE AUTHOR

Ann P. B. was a successful employee for three decades at a major company in San Diego, California. Ann excelled through the company starting in accounting, promoted to human resources, and then operations, enhancing her skills, knowledge, training, and assisting others to reach their full potentials.

The employment history was not without challenges. As difficult situations were presented, Ann would work within the company's processes and chain of command, mutually resolving issues for the well-being of her fellow employees and the company.

Ann graduated from SDSU with her BS degree in business administration and information systems. Ann's functional manager, who we will call Mark, strongly suggested Ann to apply for an open position in Supply Chain (SC) where he was the functional manager of the SC supervisor, who we will call Rick. In the SC position, due to Rick's continued unprofessional behavior and Mark's lack of proper management caused Ann to file a complaint with EEOC and later filing a lawsuit against this global corporation.

The names of the employees and the company have been changed to avoid legal issues. The information and situations that you will read in this book are true and not embellished in any form; every situation has occurred as presented. If you are faced with potential legal issues, you will read what to do and not do in pursuing your fight for justice.

PREFACE

As you continue your career in the workforce, you may be faced with adversities that are beyond your control. Working in corporate America, you will see that there are a lot of legal instabilities that are ignored or corrective action implemented depending on who you are and who favor or disfavor you in the organization.

It is imperative that you know your rights as an employee. Our legal system is not without flaws, and justice is not truly blind, so you need to help the employment lawyers enforce the very employment laws that are in existence.

If you are facing or you are a victim of wrongful termination, retaliation, salary problems, harassment, discrimination, unfair discipline, you need to read the information that is being shared in this book.

Fight for your rights and know what you need to do to be successful in your pursuit of justice.

ACKNOWLEDGMENTS

I would like to acknowledge my parents Thelma and Samuel, who are now deceased, for instilling strong work ethics and a fight for justice in my soul. Also, thanks to my husband Douglas for his support, my daughters Sheena and Angelina for their continued prayers and support, my best friend Ivey for her continued encouragement and support and always being there. My sister Evetta for the late night and early morning calls to calm me when my emotions flared up and to my late cousin Gwen who shared with me her legal knowledge of employment law.

In addition, my doctors at Kaiser and Dr. John Saint Rose, my herbalist from Blythe, California. If it were not for these individuals, I honestly do not think that I would be alive today due to the stress and the adverse reaction the situation has caused to my health. Attorney David A. Miller for providing needed information to add to this book. Always thanking God for another day when I physically was unable to get out of bed, God gave me the strength to do so.

My church family that prayed for me through the entire ordeal: Joyce, Nadi, Ivey, Pastor Greene, Rochelle my sister-in-law as well as my other circle of friends.

CHAPTER

1

Introduction
WORKING IN CORPORATE AMERICA

Working in corporate America has its positive and negative drawbacks. When seeking employment, the job seeker needs to look at the company's culture. A company that has a history of home growing their CEOs in order to maintain an ethical environment, promote employee morale, a sense of community, a team-focused environment, and respects every employee, as they would like to be respected, should be the model of all companies, but sadly, that is not always the case.

When a company's board seeks CEOs externally, it sends a very strong signal that the existing culture will be destroyed, a change in community and ethics. One has to look at how often the company has changed CEOs, the unethical behavior of the CEOs, how long that behavior was tolerated, and how long was the CEO allowed to remain in power.

When a company makes major bad choices at the board level, such as selecting one bad CEO after another, this shows that the company has become toxic and is fraught with major problems; bad management; legal issues; poor employee morale; extensive outsourcing; dismantling the company brick by brick; corruption; unprofessional behavior from the CEO, executive board, human resources, and middle management; continuous downsizing; and instability. This displays the company has a problem with direction, execution, stability, and does not respect their employees. This company will not be successful in their business matters; one day this company will cease to exist.

Before accepting employment look at the company's roadmap, look at the company's past and how drastic did it change. Change can be good with good direction, but when those that are in charge are unethical, the future will not show positive. Research how often the company downsizes, cuts salaries, restructures, continues to reorganize their organizations and continuous change in management. When a company continues to change and every change is unsuccessful, that company has major problems with management, direction, and execution. Speak with past employees, Google the company and see what information is out there, go to Glassdoor.com, do your homework to prevent an employment nightmare by joining an unstable company.

Prior to major changes bringing in external CEOs, the company's stock was as high as $120 per share; employees were very happy and gave 120 percent to the company. Management held a strong belief in community, ethics, morale, respect with a sense of loyalty. The founders of the company visited every site on a yearly basis; they reached out to every employee no matter the level. That was the company I signed up to work for, bad management was taken care of, and the system was a justifiable system and worked for the good of all employees.

All employees no matter the level shared in profit sharing, bonuses, celebrations, we had camaraderie, division review, and after the review, a company-wide beer bust. The company did not promote layoffs, employees that wanted to take advantage of early retirement or voluntary severance that was always the option. After two years, the individual could apply to come back to the company and resume employment. If these practices had never changed, the company would have still been very successful. The company believed in inventing, research, and development to answer strongly to the competition with any products that they presented to the market.

The company was known for cohesiveness, for creating an ethical environment, and it was an honor to be a part of this family. The board made a very bad decision in July 1999 to hire an outsider as the CEO of the company, knowing this outsider was about to be terminated from the previous employment.

Under this CEO, there were lawsuits for wrongful termination, unlawful discrimination, unlawful retaliation, whistle blowing, employment law violations, etc. This CEO received death threats and had armed guards. The board continued to support this CEO. This CEO would openly disrespect certain executives that raised questions and concerns; this CEO would speak over the intercom aggressively and would unprofessionally demean management as well as employees on a regular basis. Often, suppliers were on-site and witnessed the behavior. The board of directors continued to support this behavior; this CEO put executives and managers in place that behaved in the same manner. Anyone that opposed the bad behavior was terminated or forced out of the company.

This CEO introduced outsourcing, dismantling, layoffs, and the discontinuing of profit sharing. This CEO walked away from the company with more than $42 million after being fired; this CEO received bonuses upward of $13 million in profit sharing while most employees received less than 2 percent or nothing at all.

When a CEO cuts so deep into the infrastructure by outsourcing core positions, dismantling project team members that are in the heart of projects, dismantling organizations without knowing what caused its success, implementing quarterly layoffs, this is not a company that promotes solidarity, community, ethical behavior, and employee morale. Companies that exercise forced employee distribution meaning management have been demanded by the CEO and human resources to single out employees from their organization to give negative evaluations. Employees find themselves laid off, and/or demoted, this is done to prevent merit increases, or promotions in an effort to place more money back into the budget in order that executives may receive extremely high bonuses at the end of the year.

This company promotes unethical behavior from management at all levels. Employees have to be educated that human resources do not support employee concerns; human resources champion management and the company's concerns—no matter how unethical the behavior.

Performance evaluations are often fabricated to make employees work for less, feel inadequate, and to destroy the employees' self-esteem. The employee will not receive merit increase or profit sharing; top management will receive large bonuses and merit increases at the end of the year.

It is usually employees that are near retirement, people of color, and/or employees that management does not practically favor.

Management practice creating hostile environments for the employee they would like to terminate but have no grounds.

The company forces the employee to sign an agreement never to apply for employment at this company in their lifetime if the employee accepts the severance package. This policy was enforced by the CEO, supported by the board to prevent rehire of past employees who have a strong commitment to the company's past cultural environment.

The majority of these employees received great reviews, received many awards of achievement often found themselves placed in work forced distribution. Then there are those that are favored by management—missing deadlines, poor quality work, slackers, take long lunch breaks, arrive late and leave early, and disrespectful to other employees. These employees are the fabric of the company and remain employed. Not only do they remain employed, they receive promotions and bonus that others worked hard to receive. Many love triangles allow these employees to remain employed; by keeping quiet keeps a paycheck in their account.

The next external CEO the board put in place was worse than the first. One pressing message that this CEO delivered to the employees was, he did not like people and wants a lights-out company. At this point, managers shared an equal dislike for the employees they managed and respect was out the window. There were more lawsuits as well as this CEO was sued for sexual harassment from his mistress after several trips and hotel stays at the expense of the company.

The culture and community that the founders created has been totally dismantled with no trace of its existence. Management behaviors that exist now would not have been tolerated by the founders. Death came to the company with the first external CEO hired.

In companies that have noted public runs of unethical CEOs, these CEOs always put in place unethical managers, board members, vice presidents, who in turn put in place unethical lower-level managers and personnel. When those at the top practice unethical behavior, you can be sure those who report to them practice the same behavior. We had a saying at this company that bad behavior trickle from the top down into the staff, those that dare to speak up, and brown nose always remain employed.

Know whom you are reporting to

It was very important to share the background about this company so that you could see the pattern. Let's just dive into how this information will help you identify if you have a legal problem as well to look at the characteristic of those that are your managers.

Prior to graduating from SDSU, I worked in an administrative position; I worked ten years for the functional manager of finance who was later promoted to operations. Mark displayed excellent behavior during my career under him. Had it not been for me, Mark would have been terminated in 1998.

Pay close attention and (note) the signs of violations of employee rights. As you share this journey, we will use the name James for the former operations manager who was overzealous, very unethical, self-centered, and very cocky. James was attempting to secure his next position as the next general manager. His competition was Mark, and we will use the name Sam for the general manager at that time.

In order to discredit Mark and Sam, James developed a friendship with a human resource representative who we will call Mary. James started a rumor about Sam abusing drugs and making sure this information was shared with upper management. James also started the rumor that Mark, who was at that time the finance manager, was massaging the financials. Which simply means reporting numbers that was fabricated for his benefit of employment.

Between upper management and the HR representative, neither bothered to conduct a complete investigation of the accusations. They responded to the accusation as if James was God and whatever venom came out of his mouth was true. Being notified about James's plot to eliminate Mark and Sam proved to be true, I notified them of the problem. Why did James feel so comfortable in this behavior? He knew HR was corrupt and upper management was not educated in regard to employment law. Once I received the information, it was my ethical duty to share this vital information with Mark and Sam.

Sam was in disbelief because he felt James was not only his employee but also his friend since Sam hired and managed James. James was not a man of integrity, loyalty, or respect for his employees or his immediate manager. Sam hired James into the position of functional manager of operations. Putting such a scheme in place was very unethical and unprofessional but was supported by Mary in HR. James was very comfortable and felt he was untouchable. Often, James would have his administrative assistant babysit his children during work hours. She would run personal errands for him, and the sad thing is, upper management knew about it and ignored the behavior, including Mark and the general manager Sam.

Mark responded to the information that I shared and found it to be true regarding James's scheme. Mark provided information to upper management showing he did nothing wrong and was spared. Later, Mark was promoted into the position of functional manager of operations after the removal of James. Mark would not have been placed in that position if I had not warned him of the plot. Sam was terminated in front of all the employees during division review without the chance of defending himself.

An external manager from Kodak was Sam's successor as general manager. Bill was the best general manager that was put in place. He cared for the employees, personable, and Bill was very ethical.

James was later found out to have lied on Mark as well as Sam because Mary from human resource had befriended him. James would remain employed but demoted to an individual contributor. The same manager that terminated Sam in the presence of the employees was also terminated the next day in the same meeting.

What was not right in this situation? James's behavior was grounds for immediate termination: falsifying information and setting up other employees for termination and that employee happened to be the general manager.

Mary's way of handling the matter was also *unethical,* and she as well should have been terminated because she misused her authority to secure a person who violated the company's policies, procedures, and guidelines. See how Mary favoring James violated employment rights. Unethical employees often get away with bad behavior. Mary transferred, with no consequences, to Boise where she remained a human resource rep.

Sam was given a nice package in order not to sue the company once HR learned they had handled the situation extremely unprofessional. Sam had a serious medical condition that was not caused by his own doing. All of Sam's direct reports and his manager knew the situation, but since Sam was in and out of the hospital so much detoxifying to clear his system from the previous medication to start the new prescription, James took advantage of Sam's illness to remove him. If Sam had filed a lawsuit for wrongful termination, he would have walked away with more money than the company gave in his package. I would have been his strongest witness and would not have taken a pay off from the company to keep my silence.

As Mark was moved into his new position as his administrative assistant, I followed him. There was a bond of trust, and Mark knew that I was his eyes and ears.

Having sixteen years of human resource experience in multiple positions, I was able to guide Mark so that he would practice the utmost integrity, by respecting his employees, practicing model behavior, and not be a target of a lawsuit.

Roughly ten years of reporting to Mark allowed me to spread my wings. He allowed me a lot of latitude to learn, teach others, and work on major projects. I finished my education under Mark's management, receiving nice merit increases, bonuses, and recognitions and allowed to lead as well as being a member on project teams.

The trust we had was invaluable. Putting processes in place, audited department processes and systems, managed systems, database transfers, and kept the organization from being down at any given time due to systems, defected computer, or printer issues. I enjoyed going to work, making sure that everything Mark and the department needed was at their disposal without compromise.

Whenever Mark would ask an unethical question, I would caution him and provide the policy and procedures as well as employment law information that he would be breaking, which would cause legal problems. Often, he would listen. We talked about everything from our children, politics, managers, management styles, and beliefs in our faith. Mark trusted my loyalty, reliability, dependability, and the fact that I never lied to him about anything.

Mark placed me in positions such as space planner, auditor, lead administrative assistant, trainer of new employees, desk side supporter, shadow IT, webmaster, system administrative, projects, as well as the go-to person for top management to individual contributors. There was not an assignment or project given that I was not successful in completing, and completing on time or before time. Quality was never an issue; every project was documented and shared with all concerned.

Although Mark was good to me, I did often see where he was not so good to others. Often, managers that he laughed and joked with, he would often speak badly about. *Know whom you work for*, knowing that when Mark spoke badly about other managers and about their wives and children gave me serious concerns about Mark's integrity.

Mark was the functional manager of operations at this time with more or less one hundred employees that reported to him direct or indirect. He came into the organization very green; he had no clue and relied on lower-level managers already in the organization to teach him. Whenever Mark lies, he would speak quickly, skirting issues, and would not look at you eye to eye. Often I sit in on his meetings taking notes, always making sure that the information he presented was credible.

As challenging questions arise in the meeting he could not answer, he would skirt the issue, meaning he would say a lot but never answering the question.

Mark had a manager that reported to him who we will call Gloria. She was a vital asset to the department, and Mark really did not care for her and often would make negative comment as well as blonde jokes about her intellect. Gloria was highly stressed, missing a lot of work because of illness due to her workload.

During meetings, Gloria was the major person that would get under Mark's skin. Gloria would often challenge and ask the hard questions that Mark could not answer, and she often made it apparent that Mark did not know what he was talking about, and often he did not and that irritated him.

Mark requested that the staff meeting be taped and transcribed, Gloria protested with extreme concern. When questioning Mark about her concern Gloria shared,

Mark's response was "It is my staff meetings, and the meetings will be taped and transcribed until further notice." You see Mark wanted the meetings taped so that he could educate himself in areas where he was still extremely weak.

When Mark was away on a business trip in Europe, Gloria came to the desk and demanded that I do not transcribe the minutes from the meeting. She was instructed by me to send Mark an e-mail and place the request with Mark. As a manager, Gloria stated, "You are just a f——admin, and I am in charge."

The matter was reported to Mark via e-mail as well as a voice mail. Mark returned from his trip and said Gloria and I needed to work the matter out between ourselves.

That should have been the *first cue* that Mark had no backbone when it came to resolving issues. It was Mark's responsibility to reprimand Gloria because she was his employee as well as one of his managers. The matter should have been reported to HR, and there should have been a warning to Gloria. That was not done.

Gloria and I had a conversation about her unprofessional behavior. She apologized, and Mark never reprimanded her unprofessionalism or her vulgar language.

Mark complimented me for my professionalism but never handled the matter or documented the situation occurred. Mark continued taping the staff meetings for a period until others expressed their concerns.

Second cue, Mark allowed me to work on a project with business planning, due to quarter after quarter backlog report was considerably high with stock-outs. Upper management was becoming considerably concerned as well as the CEO, and customers were dissatisfied with the long turnaround on their orders. I studied the report and met with the planners. At that time the planners responsible for the report were temporary workers and did not seem too concerned. They had no loyalty to the company and knew they would never be employed.

Mark was to have a conversation with the previous planning manager who we will call JC to express management's dissatisfaction with the performance of his team.

While the conversation took place at Mark's desk, Mark did not handle the meeting as he said he would. It was extremely watered down.

JC gave his two weeks notice that he had accepted a position with the company on the East Coast. That was OK with Mark because he was not good at confrontations and was not happy with JC's department's performance.

Mark previously promised a very competent employee, who we will call Carl, that the next opened management position would be his once he finishes his master's degree. Now what I did not tell you, Mark only has a bachelor's degree in finance but often use the wager of higher education to those that he did not think would achieve the challenge in order to promote.

Third cue, Carl completed his master's well before JC gave his notice, Carl being very capable of holding the position of planning manager due to his experience in planning and his education. Mark implied the position was Carl's up to the point of his mass e-mail announcement that Rick, who no one knew anything about, was given the position.

I thought about it. If Mark would not keep his word with a trusted employee that had been under his management for so long, would he one day do the same with me? The cues were there that Mark was not honest, disloyal, unethical, and was not a man of his word. Mark lacked integrity and had no backbone and was extremely deceitful to those that supported him and helped him get to the position he is in today.

Carl was extremely disappointed, hurt, and in disbelief of the outcome, so much so that he transferred from under Mark's management to a position under the general manager. I thought back, had I not warned Mark of the plotted demise of his career, he would have been terminated with Sam. I wondered, Is he nice to me because I warned him of the plot against him? I did the right thing, but I would see him time after time lie and acquiesce when he should be standing up for what was right instead of *cowering down*.

After Mark made the offer to Rick, Mark asked if I knew anything about Rick. Carl should have been the selected choice. Since Carl was promised the position, qualified, capable, and completed his master's degree as directed by Mark. No one in the organization knew anything about Rick, and Mark did not do an investigation, requesting past evaluations or speaking with past managers to know whom he was hiring. The only thing he knew was that Rick had a master's degree. A manager of that level should have known how to run reference checks on those that he planned to hire. Mark had no clue how to run reference checks on an unfamiliar candidate.

Fourth cue, a position became opened in the department's technical section as an administrator of Windchill. I applied for the position; I had been working on projects with the section for about six months as well as auditing the Windchill systems processes. I interviewed for the position and was informed that I was the only candidate who passed the interview and would have been a great fit for the group, but the hiring manager said he was told I was no longer interested in the position.

I never shared with anyone that I was not interested; I was very interested in the position because it was in line with my degree and passion, information technology (IT). I worked close with the manager as well as the group; we had a very cohesive relation. The manager stated, "The position would have been yours if you wanted it, but we have now extended the offer to an external employee who happened to be an exiting temp from another organization." I was disappointed and inquired who would have made such a statement, and found it was a person that I worked very close with. She lied as a favor to another manager to hire this temp that was favored by her present manager. Once the lie was exposed, nothing happened to the liar because Mark was very fond of her.

Mark came to me and stated he wanted me to apply for the planning position. I shared with him I wonder who said I was not interested in the IT position; his response was, "It is water under the bridge, it is time to move forward and not focus on what could have been." Looking back, it was more likely Mark, my present manager who was also the manager over the shadow IT group Windchill, that supported the lie.

The deceit that had been witnessed about Mark's behavior with others will now turn to me. *Note:* If you see that your manager, coworker, or friend lack integrity with others, keep your eyes opened because it will definitely turn to you one day when the opportunity arise. "*Know whom you are reporting to.*" Pay attention to their character and lack of integrity toward others.

Know when you are being set up for a fall

In March 2006, Mark approached me and stated, "I want you to apply for the business planning manager's position, you have now graduated with your bachelors that I paid for, and I want you to use your degree." Being uncomfortable with the request not knowing the character of Rick, I felt I was being railroaded and the result will not be favorable for my career.

In reading my performance evaluation, Mark noted that I was required to apply for two open positions. The first position was sabotaged, and now it leaves the second position with a person I knew nothing about. I applied for the position with strong pressure form Mark. An interview was set up, and I interviewed well. I did not really expect to get the position because I felt Rick did not particularly care for me.

Mark came to our cube that we shared and asked if I had heard anything yet about the position. I stated no, and I do not think I will be selected because I do not think Rick cares for me as a person. Mark smiled and said I do not think that is true and left the area. The interview was a panel interview with five interviewers, consisting of behavioral and technical. It was later shared with me that I was the only candidate that was able to answer all the questions satisfactorily. Shortly after Mark left the area, Rick asked if he could have a word with me. We went into the conference room and Rick stated, "I would like to extend an offer to you for the business planning manager position." I was extremely shocked; it was not what I had at all expected.

The way Rick presented the offer was rough; if he was a physician, he would display terrible bedside manners.

Rick stated, "I interviewed a candidate with a master's degree, and you won over him *so consider yourself lucky.*" I should have hung on these words "*consider yourself lucky.*" What did that actually mean? Did Mark pressure Rick and made a pact with him to place me in this position? Prior to the interview, Mark communicated to Rick that he wanted more diverse hirers since the department lacked the presence of African Americans in the organization, and certainly none in management positions.

The entire situation did not feel right; *always make a mental note. If it does not feel right, it is not right.* Had I not applied, Mark would have became very negative with me, and my future would have been bleak.

Before accepting and transitioning into the new position, I had questions. I asked, "What will my transitioning salary be?" Rick stated, "You will receive half now and the second half six months later." That concerned me. I asked, "How can that be, all other employees when moving into a promotional position receive their promotional increase once the offer was accepted?"

I consulted human resources. The representative told me, HR can put in writing: "Six months after working in the position, the second half of the promotional increase will be awarded." I received the e-mail and saved it.

Note: If you are being treated differently prior to accepting a position, it will be best not to accept a position that you are being railroaded because it will not work out well for you. *Lets take a moment here.* The warning signs were flashing with *flames of fire*! The first fire spark was when *I stated, "No, and I do not think I will be selected because I do not think Rick care for me." Mark smiled and said, "I do not think that is true," and left the area.* I should have trusted my gut feeling. Second spark was when Rick stated, "*Consider yourself lucky.*" It was a warning that *I did not pick up on* that this arrangement was not going to be a union made in heaven. The third spark was when *Rick stated, "You will receive half now and the second half six months later,*" It was not a practice used with other employees in the organization.

Always get verbal promises in writing. Managers as well as HR personnel are notorious in responding, "*I do not recall making that statement or promise.*" If you do not have it in writing or an e-mail with a stamped person's name of authority, date, and time, you will lose when the manager decides he/she will not honor their word/promise.

Three weeks prior to transitioning into the position, Rick was extremely nice. You see I was also the shadow IT person in the group, as Rick was having difficulties with his laptop and printer he needed me to setup his systems and a quick lesson on how to use the HR systems for managers.

Three weeks passed and a coworker in planning whom I befriended, a new employee to the company, we will call him Ben, had a very difficult desk. Ben was not very successful in resolving the issues on his desk; he was given a free pass. You see, Ben's father was an affluent functional manager in the organization, so no matter what, Ben would be successful.

Ben passed on to me the three toughest suppliers that he managed as well as the backlog report that was severely fraught with problems. If you remember earlier, I mentioned the past planning manager was not successful in managing this backlog situation and transferred out of the organization to the East Coast, not because he could not manage, but because he knew the organization was not functionally managed well.

Well, let's continue. After Ben passed on this major headache to me, Rick called me into his office and stated, "*These suppliers as well as the backlog report is now your responsibility, and if you are not successful, it will be your job*" WOW, REALLY! That hit me out of left field. My response was "*Seriously, Ben has been managing these suppliers for a year as well as the backlog report, was he told it would be his job since he was not successful?*" Rick's response was "*FIX IT*."

Note: When situations like this happen, know that you are being set up for a fall. Document and *speak with an attorney*. I cannot impress enough of how important that will be to your case and situation as it continue to arise, because it will arise! You see, instead of me speaking with an attorney, I went to Mark because he was the functional manager, and I trusted him. I wanted to use the chain of command. Mark asked me to trust him to speak with Rick. I trusted him when I should not have. Always remember that the manager is strictly for the company and not for you, the employee.

It is important to share with an attorney about the conversations, e-mails, behaviors as well as suspicions so that you can be instructed properly how to document chains of events.

You also want to be instructed what to watch for in behavior, and what to do and not do. Never become insubordinate. Complete your tasks and projects on time or before time.

Make sure you produce quality work. Do not do anything that your manager can come back and say that you were unprofessional in any manner even though a lying manager will fabricate every situation that you are involved. Because he/she is a manager, the word of a manager will be believed over a subordinate every time. Know that it is your side, the manager's side and the truth.

This information that is being shared with you is very valuable; so many employees are facing these situations as this book is being written. I am providing you with tools that you would never otherwise receive from anyone else. Consult with EEOC as well as a qualified employment attorney that would not be afraid to go up against a corporate giant. You will see giants will eventually fall.

Let's continue. I took the challenge with no other choice. As I begin the project of investigating the root cause of the grossly backlog situation, I had to develop relationships with my counterparts in Europe, Asia, United States, Canada, and Mexico.

As the relationships were being built, Rick sent e-mails to some of my contacts and instructed them to push back on all my requests. *Why*, I was leading the project. I was developing my team with three months to completion. Rick's desire was to see me fail the project and terminate me instead of resolving the stock-out problem.

In other words, Rick sent the message to some of my team that stated, "*Do not work with her, nor give her information she may request.*" I had *three months* to turn this mess around, and it was becoming extremely difficult until my Asian and European counterpart sent me a copy of Rick's e-mail.

The European counterpart came to the United States for a week to work with the group. As we had our one-on-one, he shared that it was pleasant working with me face to face and that he was sorry for being so harsh "*but that is the way we Germans are and the fact that Rick instructed me to push back on your requests was causing problems in the supply chain.*"

After our relationships became more cohesive, we came up with a way to keep Rick out of our conversations to repair the problem in the supply chain. I was able to discover the root cause of the backlog issue. With the team, we developed a very strong relationship, and as the leader of this project having a solid team behind me globally, we were able to put processes in place. I successfully received management support in Asia, Europe, and the Americas to correct the backlog problem.

Instead of Rick being pleased with the accomplishment, he showed irritation. I worked with my international team and found glitches in the MRP system that was also causing planning issues. The information was shared with Rick and the administrator of the MRP system. With a team effort for my global counterparts and my IT supporter found a remedy that would allow the group to be more productive and tweak the system to work as it was designed.

Rick reviewed the information, and when he saw it would add success to the challenges he assigned me, it would prove more success, more latitude to be successful. Rick denied the proposed solution. Rick knew that it would make not only my job harder by denying the system adjustment but the other planners as well. Rick was simply sabotaging the progress and success of the planning group.

At this point, the confirmation was made; Rick continued to exercise his plan for termination. The end of the quarter came, and I accomplished the backlog issue, put processes in place, and shared the success with upper management. By June, the interaction between Rick and I became very strained. Rick would send not so tasteful e-mails, and I saved them on my company laptop as well as forwarding them to my home e-mail account.

At this point, to have an attorney that was instructing how to handle this situation would have been extremely beneficial. Employees should know their employment rights. Let's continue because at this point it is just bad management in the eyes of the law. Rick broke policies, guidelines, and procedures; you will see when bad management turns into violating employment rights.

Working twelve to thirteen hours most days to stay ahead of the workload managing the three largest suppliers and Rick not allowing adjustments to the MRP system was causing a lot of manual work to keep threats from becoming a reality with supply planning and the backlog report.

KB was the SAM of one of the suppliers I managed. This supplier had been shipping damaged products to the distribution center. After an investigation with logistics as well as the supplier, it was apparent that the damage was caused by the supplier. KB, the supply alliance manager (SAM), was also to be investigating the situation.

I requested KB to join me for a teleconference with the supplier. As the meeting progressed, KB stated to the supplier, "*You do not need to listen to her [meaning me] she is new to the position so she does not know what is going on.*" This was her way of discrediting me. After the meeting, I asked the SAM if she thought her behavior was professional. Discrediting a coworker in the presence of the supplier is not only unprofessional but also demeaning. I also showed her the photos of damaged goods leaving the supplier's facility.

KB started yelling and continued behaving unprofessionally. The conversation with her was "*You are yelling, I cannot hear you, and you will not hear what I have to say. Once you calm down, we can speak on Monday.*"

This is now six months into the business planning position. I reported the incident to Rick, and he stated, "*I will speak with her.*" I also asked Rick, "*are you happy with my performance so far.*" Rick's response, "*I am pleased, keep up the good work.*" Now what I am about to tell you next was *a violation of my employment rights.*

CHAPTER

2

The Evaluation

It is Monday; it is time to receive my evaluation as well as my promotional increase. KB came to my desk and apologized for her behavior, stating she was really stressed and experiencing PMS. I accepted her apology. Rick came to my desk and asked me to come with him to the conference room. As we were walking, he was very arrogant and unfriendly. Evaluations are always done in private at the company, and normally, the manager is pleasant despite if the evaluation is negative or positive.

We arrived to the conference room. As I sat down, POUND! Rick slammed his hand down on the table, making a loud noise, pointing his finger in my face as he threw my evaluation across the table, *yelling*, "You *are a problem.*"

As I spoke with my attorney after the fact, that is considered a *verbal assault. This is a violation of employment law.* I was stunned, not aware what had just happened. I felt a spear go right through my heart. Was there something I missed? Rick just told me on Friday to keep up the good work. I shared the KB situation, and he said he would speak with her.

I started thinking back over the last six months. I made all my deadlines despite how difficult Rick made the challenge, and I had no issues with my coworkers since I worked 95 percent with my international team.

They sent me copies of their 360-degree feedbacks that were sent to Rick.

I read through the evaluation, and it was great, then I read the feedback, and it did not match with the e-mails that were sent to me from my team.

Rick had in the feedback KB was angry with me and I was accused of acting unprofessional with her. I defended myself by stating, "This did not what happened," and asked, "Did KB tell you she came and apologized?" His response was "No, I did not know." He also stated that it was reported that I made changes to the MRP system that caused issues with planning and that is unacceptable. I stated, "That is incorrect," and shared with him TS made the changes. Since the problem was caused by TS, Rick's favored employee, it was now considered a system error and nothing serious. When he thought it was my error, it was unacceptable and corrective action would be exercised.

Then he stated, "I am ranking you a *one*, and you will not receive your promotional increase." (*To deny an employee of their promotional increase is a violation of employment rights.*) It was good that I kept the e-mail from six months prior; *you will want to know how this was handled.* Rick went further, stating, "*Your coworkers do not like you, and you have the communication skills of a two-year-old.*" "*I want you to ask your coworkers why they do not like you and what you can do to make them like you.*" "*I want you to take communication workshop.*" "*Further, I do not care what your coworkers say or do to you, if you say anything they do not like, I will physically escort you out of the facility myself.*" Rick began creating a hostile environment for me in the work place.

Allowing his hatred for me due to my nationality had totally polluted his way of thinking. This is what caused individuals to become disgruntled.

What was violated in this meeting?
- Unfair discipline.
- Refusing to honor the commitment of the promotional increase, which would fall into pay problems?

Those of you that are experiencing issues with your manager or someone in authority, when they suggest a closed room for a meeting, strongly request an open environment to avoid abusive behavior. If you are forced into a closed room and you have experienced unprofessional behavior in the past, speak loud enough for someone to hear you, speak clearly, which will force your manager to speak louder, the opportunity will provide witness that may have heard the conversation, be sure to document and contact your attorney. As you gather witnesses, *have a witness that is not a part of your department and may be going through a similar situation.*

Select someone that cannot be bought off by the company, someone that cannot be paid to lie. Clearly, I removed myself from the situation and took a walk. After the walk, I sent Mark an e-mail about the entire situation. Mark skirted the issue, stating, "I will give you an e-award to try and compensate you. I was already losing $500 a month going into this position without the increase due to working overtime.

I notified Mark and Rick that this issue will be taken up with HR. The promise was made by HR, Mark, and Rick. Interesting enough, they all stated that no such promise was made (*lies*).

I expected them to lie, and now the e-mail came in handy. The complaint was filed with HR; I filed it with the VP of HR. I received a response, and the investigation started. The e-mail that was received from HR was forwarded to the HR investigators.

It took two months for HR to conclude their investigation. The conclusion: what Rick was attempting to do was illegal. Rick refused to give me my merit increase that I deserved and did not deserve to be ranked 1. Three months later, HR instructed

Rick to do a second ranking review where my rank was raised because there was no justification for the previous ranking. Employees reported that Rick was soliciting negative information about me in order to terminate me. James displayed this same behavior with Sam in 2000.

Also investigated were the people that Rick stated he received the 360-degree feedback. Once the employees turned in their feedback, they were told, "Now tell me something that she need to improve on." When he did not get what he wanted, he solicited feedback from others that I did not interact with in the course of my job.

HR granted the promotional increase and the retaliation began.

Retaliation is violation of employment law. Examples of retaliation will be very clear; I have now been in the position for nine months and just received my promotional increase. I did receive the e-award from Mark to make up for the lost months. That was Mark throwing a bone to keep my trust because now he wanted me out as much as Rick because I dared to go to HR and win and now the conspiracy starts. One reason why the investigation went well, the rep that led the charge was very ethical, and complete.

After she concluded that it was unlawful what Rick was doing, she left the company taking early retirement.

Rick decided to assign a lead planner to the group when issues or approvals for air shipment needed to be granted this planner would sign off. The lead planner was just as rude and unprofessional as Rick, still being responsible for the backlog; the lead planner stated, "*You are also responsible for the other planner's errors in this report!*"

Red alerts were blowing up through out this ordeal.

The lead planner stated, "*As planners submit their numbers, you better scrub the backlog and make sure the numbers are right because you own it.*"

Not only did the lead planner make me responsible for other's errors, he also set a deadline that was unrealistic. Ben was not held accountable for others' errors, so now the game has changed, Ben is no longer in the crosshairs; I have just been put in place to catch the bullet. The stress started becoming insurmountable; I felt my body quaking as if an earthquake was erupting in my soul. Illness started consuming my body, but not once did I miss coming into work nor did I miss deadlines.

We are now a few months into 2007; I have been completely successful in my projects, deadlines, and the impossibilities that Rick placed on my desk. Rick supported the lead planner in all his unprofessional decisions. I discussed the issues with Rick. Rick responded, "*This lead planner will be successful at all cost.*" The employment situation started becoming a major nightmare.

I received MD's information for the backlog report, and the entire report she submitted was incorrect. MD is one of the domestic planners. I went to Rick and asked if he would ask the entire planning team to double-check their sources and submit clean reports. Rick stated he would but the conversation never took place. This went on for two months; Rick sent me an e-mail that the report needed to be sent to him by 12:00 noon every Tuesday. Minutes later, MD notified me that she has more important things to do and her report will not be on time. She stated Rick has extended the deadline.

I was extremely frustrated and said to MD I have yet to receive a clean report on time from anyone. I managed to hold my composure. My frustration I shared is truly with Rick's lack of communication, support, and honesty. I asked Rick for a meeting. He put me off and avoided me until the next morning. When he came into the office Wednesday morning, I swear he smelled of alcohol masked with breath freshener. I had been to the doctor the previous Friday. I had been coughing up blood. My voice was extremely raspy, and I was having difficulty speaking and swallowing and experienced continuous pain in my chest (stress).

Rick came to my desk and said, "Let's go into a conference room for this meeting." I thought he was going to acknowledge my request in speaking with MD in regard to her errors.

As we walked, Rick stated, "What is wrong with your voice, did you lose it from yelling?" I had no idea what he was talking about since I was unable to speak clearly for a few weeks, I shared that I have been having issues with my throat and experiencing bleeding and pain for quite a while.

We arrived in the silo room in an adjoining building. Rick's hand slapped the table like a crazy fool, ears red as fire, and eye's glazing as if he was insane, finger about an inch from my face. Spit flying as he was yelling, anyone in the vicinity could have heard him. He yelled, "*You insulted a coworker in a public setting, and I will not tolerate that from no one. You had her crying, and she came to me and said you were condescending and rude, you better never talk to her again. I will throw you out of here so fast you won't know what hit you. You could be heard yelling across the building!*"

VERBAL ASSULT! ILLEGAL! Not OK!

I spoke and told Rick, "*It never happened. I have been experiencing esophageal spasms, bleeding, and pain I cannot yell. I have been to the doctor and tests are being conducted to figure out why I am experiencing this problem.*" Rick continued to pour out the insults; this man is a fool and a racist bigot. His hatred for my nationality of people pour so deep in his veins that no hope or reasoning would ever prevent him from his goal and that is to terminate me. Rick has no heart, ethics, and he hosts a demonic soul.

I asked Rick, "*Do you think the way you are speaking to me right now is professional or even appropriate?*" Rick stated, "*Yes, as long as it is done privately, I can talk to you however I want.*" Then the insults started again. "*You have the IQ of a two-year-old, you will never be successful, and you better be concerned about your career at the company.*" I shared, "*A two-year-old could never accomplish what I have accomplished. A two-year-old would never get a college degree, nor could a two-year-old meet and exceed his challenges and sabotages you brought my way.*"

I asked Rick if he is practicing bigotry, and he looked at me dumbfounded and stated, "If you talk to the MD, you will be fired."

I went on to tell Rick, "*You speak to me as a slave master speaks to his slave on the plantation.*" I also asked, "*Why did you hire me into this position since you hate me so much?*" I responded to Rick, "*Your communication style is lacking the professionalism that you are supposed to promote.*" Rick stated, "If you say anything to any one about this, it will be your job."

Note: *If your manager is verbally or physically abusive, it is illegal for him/her to demand you keep the matter silent.* Document the situation, date, time, what was said, demeanor, and contact your attorney for advise. HR and upper management will take the manager's position. No matter if they know the complaint is true, they will do it to weaken any lawsuit case that may arise. Management and HR fear that if they do not take the manager's position, a lawsuit against the company is imminent. Make sure you have witnesses. If you tape the conversation, illegal taping is a $5,000 fine for each conversation taped. If the company later sues you, it will allow the tapes to be admitted into evidence to prove your case. You decide if you want to tape or not. Taping will diffidently prove the manager is a liar.

I asked Rick, "*How possible is it for me not to speak to MD, I am the project lead of the backlog report, loss of supplies, and the obsolesces report.*" I requested him to take away the backlog report and give it to MD or even VK since he so highly favor them. Rick refused because I made the request.

I spoke with MD and shared what Rick stated that I upset her to the point of tears. MD stated she never went to Rick, Rick came to her, and she stated the situation never happened as he shared. She stated I told him you shared your frustration of his lack of communication and support. Rick fabricated the entire incident, and Mark bought into it hook, line, and sinker. Mark said to me, "Of course, MD would deny what she said to keep the peace. **WOW**, how ignored are those that are placed at the top."

I asked Rick, "*Are you angry because you had to retract the evaluation and honor the promotional increase.*" He stated, "Be concerned about your career here at the company."

(*An attorney could have really assisted at this point. My mistake was trusting Mark. Note: management and HR are strictly for the company. I cannot share this point enough, and they are not for the employee. They will lie, sabotage, and use their deep pockets to pay witnesses off, in some cases even judges.*)

In immediately speaking with Mark and sharing Rick is a bigot and is setting me up for termination, Mark stated, "No, I don't think so, he has communication and interpersonal issues, you should know he is being coached by me." Mark stated, "Bear with me and everything will be OK." When you think you are being discriminated against, it is best to **have an attorney** to consult with. If I had that at this point, I would not have gone through four years of hell and damaged my health working in this organization and with these unethical managers.

I requested a meeting with Rick and Mark. I wrote out the incidence, even the fact that Rick and the lead planner SJ stated that I was responsible for other's errors in the backlog report, Rick's lack of professionalism, his racist behavior, as well as his physical threats and consistent threats of terminating my employment along with his derogatory e-mails.

Mark made a statement to Rick in these words, "*If she fell, you fell.*" Mark did not mean a word of what he stated to Rick, "*Rick is trying to help you be successful, just give him a chance.*" I stated, "He is a bigot." Mark cautioned me again to watch my words. Mark also strongly advised me to get rid of the e-mails because as he stated, it is baggage, and the meeting was soon called to an end.

At this point, I have already reported to Mark twice that Rick is a bigot, as well as sharing supporting behavior concerns and e-mails. Mark's responsibility as the functional manager was to report the complaint to HR. When any employee makes such an allegation of racism about a manager, it is the responsibility of the functional manager to document and report the matter to HR. That never happened. Mark requested patience, and he will work everything out. Let me remind you that this is 2007.

I continued to work hard, work on projects, and receive threats about my job from Rick. Rick's hatred was so strong that he could not see my intellect or contributions because he could not get past the fact that I am an intelligent person of color. Rick is guilty of retaliation, harassment, and racism but protected by Mark and the company.

Retaliation

Information provided by the Law Offices of David A. Miller: Quite often, you will do or say things you believe are appropriate and fair. It may be something like *reporting harassment of unfair treatment*. It may mean asking to see a doctor when you have been hurt at work. It can also mean sticking up for a coworker who is being treated unfairly or insisting on your overtime pay, or *pay that is due you.*

Most employers will respond fairly and appreciate your actions. Some will not. Some employers will retaliate by cutting your hours, *overloading your work, harassing you*, demoting, or transferring you or your position, *criticizing you unfairly* or even terminating you.

Retaliation is illegal

The first two chapters of this book alert you of retaliatory behavior from an individual that has been placed in a management position. Rick's behavior was reported to Mark the functional manager who is also Rick's manager as well as my former manager. Following the chain of command, the company expects the first complaint to be shared with the individual's manager, then his manager's manager, and finally HR.

- ✓ Harassment and unfair treatment reported to Mark, Rick's immediate manager.
- ✓ Pay that was due to me reported to Rick, Mark, and HR.
- ✓ Overloaded with work and unfair deadlines assigned by Rick.
- ✓ Harassment, yelling, and verbal assaults in conference rooms, threatening terminations continuously: "*Be concerned about your career with the company.*"
- ✓ Unfair criticism: "*The IQ of a two-year-old, your coworkers do not like you.*"
- ✓ Creating a hostile environment to make it impossible for the employee to perform required duties.

These behaviors display retaliation. *Consult employment attorneys, keep a record* of *all e-mails, secure a viable witness.*

In the end of 2007, an old coworker LM who knew Rick a few years back contacted me. It had been about three years since any communication. I told LM, whom I now report to, and he could not believe Rick was still employed. Rick was once a manager and was demoted because of lack of people and communication skills as well as unprofessional behavior.

Rick worked from home for a period of years. Instead of the company terminating him, he was lightly reprimanded and should not have been able to become a manager again without the proper training.

How effective is training if the trainee practices racial discrimination? He/she will not see past the color of an individual's skin of a particular nationality. We are not in slavery times, but there are a growing number of individuals that feel superior over another because of their skin color. These people are often protected. You see, when you see a company that weed through their employee bank and never promote into management African Americans and continue to terminate this nationality of people this states that racism is still alive and well in the United States. Slavery was not abolished in their minds and practices. Individuals and companies will do whatever it is to prevent African Americans and/or women from breaking through that glass ceiling.

Discrimination

Discrimination is illegal in hiring practices or in the workplace. The same reasons listed under harassment also apply to discrimination. Discrimination also includes the following:

- ✓ Disability relating to HIV and AIDS
- ✓ Requesting family care leave

✓   Requesting leave for your own serious health condition
✓   Requesting pregnancy disability leave

Direct evidence of discrimination is rare. Employers do not usually write down a plan to discriminate or tell people about a plan to discriminate. The courts understand this type of illegal activity is usually proven by circumstantial evidence.

When the employer terminates you for a discriminatory reason, but gives you a false reason, discrimination can be easier to prove. Then you do not have to prove discrimination was the only reason for termination.

You only have to prove discrimination was a "motivating factor" in the termination decision. This is easier to prove in most cases.

As we move into 2008, we have a better handle with the backlog report; the issue that remains is MD still submits her report full of errors. I requested Rick to assign the report to someone else, and he refused because I made the request.

I started having major challenges with my health. My hair started falling out, turning gray like overnight, and I was losing blood. I went to many doctors, and they could not figure out what was wrong with me other than major stress. I started having fainting spells, bruising for no apparent reason, weakness, muscle and joint pains.

I shared with Rick my health issues, and he piled on the stress. The stressors were not the job. The stress was Rick, and he was very subtle with his discrimination since I have now complained twice to Mark. I shared with my coworker Ben about Rick's racist behavior. Ben was a major brown nosier; Rick would invite part of the team to personal functions. Ben came in one morning and stated, "Rick is a f——racist, I am sorry, but he is a bigot." Ben would deny he made the statement later when I filed a lawsuit and called him as a witness.

In November I was diagnosed with leukopenia. It was severe. I shared this information with Mark and Rick. Rick would have been happy if I died. Why do I say that? It is because his behavior became worse.

When it came to being a witness, Ben lied and said he did not recall the conversation. Rick continued to sabotage my projects and tasks, continued telling my coworkers they did not have to give me reports, and telling managers in Asia not to work with me. Mark was a part of the setup. He knew about Rick's behavior and chose to assist instead of prevent. I asked Rick again if he was a racist, and he looked at me like a deer looking into high-beam headlights.

I asked Rick if he had ever managed a person of my nationality. He stated no. I went on to ask if he had ever attended a meeting where my nationality was in charge. He said no. I asked if he ever associated with people of my nationality or his friends. He said no.

Then I asked, "*How can you manage me if you cannot look past the color of my skin.*" He did not respond. I asked Rick to ask his friends how they felt about people of my nationality. He said he would and he would get back with me. He never did. Legally, the bigots know how to stay below the radar.

Bigots can get away with their bigotry in the workplace, in the courts, and in their communities. I try and believe in the law, but justice is not blind, justice is very partial. When you work for a company that promotes and protects people of this behavior, you must document, document, document. I will encourage you *not* take the law into your own hands that will only compile the problem. Even though our legal system is severely flawed, it is what we have. Document, have those of your friends to put in writing what they have witnessed, so later they cannot recant their statement.

File a complaint with EEOC, and then file a complaint with your HR department *in that order*. Only speak with upper management once. If nothing is done, you can trust they will do nothing to the rogue manager, and you have just been targeted for termination. If you go to HR before going to EEOC, the HR department will protect the manager and turn the table on the employee. When the bigots tell you not to discuss your concerns with anyone else, that is when you make sure you report in a document format provided by your attorney, preferably e-mails because of date, time stamp, to and from is documented. The law looks for the smoking gun; what did he say or do that was discriminatory? If your manager or employees assault you, let them and file assault charges with your local police department in order to start tracking the incident.

It takes an extremely ignored person that believes his/her nationality is superior over another. Racism is spewed by evilness, one that has a hunger for power, not satisfied in their skin or life situation.

A bigot is worse than a cobra snake spewing its venom out to those that are weak minded that will fall into their belief or behavioral pattern. There is only one race, and that is the human race. All nationalities still fall into the human race.

Fight against racism. Racism is not an acquired skill; it is bad behavior, get evidence, witnesses, documents, and the law. Confront bigotry; let him/her know that this behavior is unacceptable and that you will take legal actions. It takes one person at a time to abolish this behavior.

Chapter

3

Harassment

We all know harassment is not allowed at work. Harassment is illegal no matter what, especially if it is because of the following:

- ✓ Sex (gender)
- ✓ Race
- ✓ Color
- ✓ Religion
- ✓ Sexual orientation
- ✓ Martial status
- ✓ National origin
- ✓ Ancestry
- ✓ Disability—physical or mental
- ✓ Cancer or cancer-related conditions
- ✓ Age
- ✓ Pregnancy, childbirth, or related conditions

Sexual harassment does not have to be outright sexual in nature. It can include intentional staring or just interfering with your work because of your gender. One court found that stuffing paper into the squad car's shotgun barrel was an act of sexual harassment against the female police officer. A wide variety of misbehavior can be sexual harassment.

Sexual orientation includes heterosexuality, homosexuality, and bisexuality. You cannot be harassed because of your sexual preferences.

Your employer must take action to prevent harassment. This includes having a policy against harassment. The policy must be more than just giving you a written handbook that says harassment is not allowed. A real policy must actually be enforced, not just written on paper.

The employer must also take immediate appropriate corrective action if a harassment compliant is made. The action taken must be strong enough to make sure the harassment stops. The employer must protect you from any retaliation for making a complaint.

Mark failed me, HR failed me. Now it is 2008. Barack Obama won the presidency. A lot of employees were very happy of all nationalities. Managers in our department were very unhappy; the entire climate became worse in behavior. Comments like, we are not ready for a black president, and this country is going to hell in a hand basket. Some coworkers and friends were extremely happy that President Obama won, but only one manager in the organization felt as we did because he voted for him as well.

Management throughout the company showed their disappointment, and it was taken out on the employees of color. We were targeted for termination; one by one, we were being removed from the organization as well as the company. Management would state positions are being eliminated or outsourced, and right away, you would see the position being filled with an employee not of color. Our positions were being posted, and we were made to interview for positions we worked in for years.

This was what is called the Obama backlash. Anyone that looks like Obama was targeted for termination, and that practice is still moving forward at the company today in 2011.

Being the shadow IT person for the organization, the IT group notified me of server replacements. The old servers will be replaced with blade servers. That meant the databases SC use would need to be migrated to the blade servers. As I started scheduling and notifying all concerned, Rick told me my coworker VK, a person without IT experience, would take the migration lead.

I explained the problem would be a failure in the systems if he enforces that decision. VK started asking me for information as to what need to be done. My response to her, "You need to ask Rick." Rick was pressing me to do the job, but VK would get the credit. I refused. VK shared with Rick that she cannot do it; she does not have an IT background. At that point, Rick instructed me to continue leading the project. It is very disheartening that an individual could be so ignorant to the needs of the organization that he failed to realize that knowledge, experience, and execution is needed to keep an organization running.

Rick truly did not conceive the concept of project management; he would sabotage any project that I was leading or a member just to discredit my ability to perform the job.

Rick continued to take projects that I started and give to others in the middle of the project. Rick had no IT background and did not have a solid understanding of business planning; he depended on the planners to educate him.

Rick and Mark promoted the logistic person GP to head planner. In the staff meeting, GP stated, "*I've been promoted to the position, I do not know what I am doing so go figure.*" Rick put her over projects that I implemented and executed, and for the first time the projects slipped the completion schedule. I saw the system flow chart that GP tried to put together. She was missing key steps, and I did not share it with her because she lacked integrity and respect for members of the group. She was allowed to bully and mimic the character of Rick.

You see if there was no tracking or documentation that we were working on projects or completed projects, our ranking drops. Rick said to me, "You are to make GP the lead planner successful at all cost." The "all cost" would be my position. She did not have the knowledge or experience for planning nor IT, and she was placed as lead.

Rick also brought in another planner into the organization, the one that I mentioned earlier that Rick said I embarrassed in a public setting MD. In order for me to get the job, I had to have a bachelor's degree as well as experience. This planner had neither a degree nor experience; she had the same skin color as Rick so that was pleasing to him. MD lacked knowledge and experience that is why all the reports she turned into was full of errors. I am not saying MD is not intelligent, but I am saying MD lacked the experience needed when it came to business planning how to execute, investigate, and follow through.

Rick brought in a third person, LL, into the position of business planner. She had no experience, but she had a degree, I believe, in marketing. Both of these people were not people of color and were given a free pass to do what they wanted without following SC processes and procedures.

I was the only employee that was held to the policy, guidelines, and regulations. GP and the LL could act unprofessionally, miss deadlines, turn in substandard reports, and they were not held to any rules under Rick's and Mark's management. On the contrary, they were encouraged not to work with me as well as make my job as difficult as possible, and that, they did. When LL would make a drastic error, she never took accountability; she would always respond that's how you trained me. I kept a training log and documented the processes and procedures that were given to LL, and her response was "Oh, I guess I misunderstood" and that was acceptable to Rick.

As mentioned earlier, I managed the end-of-life products. As products were becoming obsolete, a year prior, I would send the trigger to my suppliers, global planners, management, as well as our marketing employees. Rick had Ben to identify SKUs to build buffer stock to be held at the supplier we met weekly. Ben had made his selection. As products came up for obsolesces, I shared that information in these meetings.

In addition, I would send an e-mail out to Rick, Ben, and anyone else that had a need to know. Rick gave the approval to Ben to start building buffer stock. I saw two SKUs on the list that was set for obsolesces and brought it to Rick's and Ben's attention for a second time. Rick responded, "I thought we had come to an agreement of the products to be produced, and if you are not on board with the plan I will relieve you from this position and the team." I produced an e-mail that I sent earlier listing the SKUs that were targeted for obsolescence that were overlooked by Rick and Ben.

These products were given to Ben as well as Rick at the last meeting; Ben was responsible in taking them off the list. I raised the question with Rick: Would you rather build buffer stock for products that were coming to end of life and end up scrapping millions of dollars worth of inventory? If you select to build, you are the manager, and you will make the call. I made sure that this was sent by e-mail.

I received a response back from Rick, stating, "*You should be more convincing when trying to make a point.*" It has always been apparent that no matter what or how I did my job, Rick would continue to make it difficult. I truly began to understand why earlier in Rick's career he was removed from management. However, at that time his previous manager did not take the time to terminate him. A bad apple was placed back into the mix to continue to contaminate the entire barrel. Neither Rick nor Ben took responsibility for the blunder. Rick played it off by saying, "*I should have been more convincing.*" Ben did come and thanked me for pointing out the problem so that he would not make such an expensive mistake.

The difference in treatment was apparent. We had weekly staff meetings. During round table, each employee state what they are working on without interruption. Rick would call on each of us. Everyone spoke in depth the pros and cons of their tasks. When Rick called on me and as I spoke about what I was working on, he would ask other employees to make decisions on work that I am responsible for, mainly TS and MD. When I would object because it was not the right decision for the success of my responsibilities, he would roll his eyes and state I was not open to others' opinions. He never solicited opinion for others deliverables. He would allow them to do their jobs the way they seen fit.

Rick started labeling me as being difficult, continued to tell others to push back on my request, and tell me I have no right to request information from others, which I needed to complete my deliverables. Rick forced me to follow the recommendation of those employees, and when it failed, he demanded I fix it because "*the responsibility belongs with you and not your coworkers.*" Rick's entire management style was unorthodox, unethical, and extremely unprofessional. If Rick could not destroy me one way, he would try another.

I know there are many of you going through the same thing from your employer despite your nationality. In my situation, Rick happens to be a bigot. In your situation, it may be something different. Just know it is never OK to be harassed or bullied from any individual no matter his or her status. Bullying leads to disgruntled employees, and disgruntled employees often go postal. *Note it is also not OK for you to become physically aggressive against someone that is harassing you.* Work through the legal system and pray that justice will prevail. Always know unethical behavior can only last a short time. It will end. We all get what is due whether good or bad, and we all get what is due.

The employer is responsible for preventing harassment—that means human resource and upper management—but Rick and Mark were the promoters of harassment. The work environment is not supposed to be hostile or toxic. When this happens, document and inform those in the area and in other areas that you can trust to periodically come to your area to observe the behavior. Do not keep unprofessional behavior to yourself. That is how those that practice it become successful in their conquest. If you can tape their conversations, it will prove valuable later.

Rick would conduct one-on-ones with all who reported to him. During our one-on-ones, he would ask what positions interest me for the future. I stated NPI or forecasting. I have mastered planning, and investigation of planning wrote procedures, etc. Rick gave the opportunity to VK who had not mastered strategic planning and had human relation issues. I had a professional relationship with my coworkers while VK always miss deadlines with no consequences as well as her personality was consistently volatile.

SL the female forecaster in the group had formed a close relationship with me. We were like sisters. Rick at the time was crude and harsh with SL; he gave VK the long-term forecast duties. As she failed the deadline, SL and VK became very irate with each other.

VK began swearing and yelling at me as well as SL. Rick heard the entire ordeal. Rick asked me to take VK outside and calm her down. Remember, when Rick yelled and behaved very unprofessionally and said this behavior would not be tolerated, he threatened to physically throw me out so fast that I would not know what hit me. VK, who is not a person of color, could curse, yell, and behave unseemly and nothing happens.

How could a major corporation allow such behavior from their managers and support them in their employment. This is not an isolated incident at this company. Many people of color or less favored by management have been treated with malicious behavior, and because they are not of color, it is allowed all the way up the chain of command. *Remember the information that I shared about the two external CEOs that were hired into the company and how long they were able to behave unethically.*

It trickles down from the top and contaminates the entire pool of managers; this practice is permitted at this company.

Rick became very close with VK; she was continuously taking vacations. They would secretly meet for lunch. When she was not on vacation, she was on disability or calling in sick. She continued to be MIA and was always missing deadlines. Why was the treatment so different? I was a top-notch employee, loyal to a fault, committed, dependable, always delivered on time, and helped my fellow coworkers to excel in their positions. Despite the crude treatment, I made Rick and Mark look very good.

When harassment is approved in a company that is fraught with unethical behavior, where those in power feel superior, they become comfortable in their behavior. We live in an environment where companies practice the right to work. They will go through any length to destroy a life.

Unethical behavior:
1. Not conforming to approved standards of social or professional behavior.
   a. Unethical business practices
      i. (Wrong) Contrary to conscience or morality or law
      ii. (Ethical) Conforming to accepted standards of social or professional behavior
2. Not adhering to ethical or moral principles.
   a. Dishonorable; immoral; unethical base; dishonorable
   b. Dishonorable in thought and deed
      i. Cowardly or treacherous
      ii. Having little or no integrity
      iii. Unworthy and despicable
      iv. Use of conduct; characterized by dishonor
      v. Deceptive or fraudulent, disposed to cheat or defraud or deceive
      vi. Lacking in value or merit
      vii. Violating principles of justice
      viii. Completely lacking nobility in character or quality or purpose
      ix. Lacking respectability in character or behavior or appearance

In your experience with your manager, do you see any of these characteristics? A disturbing thought is these people think it is OK because this behavior is ingrained into the very fabric of their lives. These individuals should never be placed in charge of another human being.

CHAPTER

4

Unfair Discipline

As the years progress and Rick is very comfortable in his unethical behavior, we move into 2009. Rick started the discussion of outsourcing a portion of the planners' positions. The first discussions were to outsource the backlog report, and value packs, NPI, forecasting, and weekly planning had not been thrown into the plan at this meeting.

GP was placed as the project manager. She was asked to find ways of leveraging. At the next meeting, Rick asked our opinion about how we felt about the outsourcing/ offshoring. Our Virginia office and Asia office also were involved in the conversation. Everyone gave his or her opinion negative and positive; everyone was concerned and wanted to know what this would look like.

The Virginia office was very vocal. As I watched Rick's response, he showed empathy and assured them that something would work out. The local planners also stressed their concerns; MD and LL were very concerned and vocal in their comments. It was my turn to speak; my question was have the individuals from India been trained and able to take the challenge. The suppliers are fraught with serious issues so what is that going to look like.

Empathy left Rick's face. His comment was "Are you saying you are opposed to the outsourcing?"

Rick did not make such a comment to any of the other planners, and my concerns were very appropriate. GP's comment was we are doing research and speaking with other organizations that have outsourced. My next question, "When and what will be going to India, and how will they be trained?" Valid questions that could not be answered at that time. The plan had not been well thought out at this point.

I was later told by Rick, "*You will not be a part of the training since you are opposed to the offshoring.*" If I had said nothing, then I would have been told that I refuse to participate or offer assistance. **Unfair discipline**, in chapter 3, the definition of unethical behavior has been broken down to display such personality.

This was the forming of a project team; Rick knew that my input was valid. In the company, there were organizations bringing back duties for India due to the lack of technical experience. There were at least twenty individuals involved in this meeting, and I was the only one who had composure, the only person of color, and the only one that was singled out.

As I was not to be part of the training, that was OK with me. I had the most complicated suppliers; these suppliers were large, produced the largest amount of products for the company, and yield the most revenue. There were a lot of quality, delivery, demand issues with these suppliers that could not be corrected in a short period.

Rick approached me and said, "Your suppliers will not be outsourced until all the issues are resolved." Rick hated the fact that an intelligent female of color knew more than he. He should have been used to my knowledge. It was not about us as individuals; it was about how we could benefit the company.

I was informed by the engineers that worked with my European supplier; this supplier had decided to open a facility in the United States on the East Coast. We were tasked with separating the defined products in the SC that will be produced in Europe and what would be produced in America. While focus needed to be placed on this new request, GP sent a request that she needed information on each supplier—SKU numbers, lead-time, pallet size, regions and contacts to be populated in a spreadsheet she designed to launch her offshoring project.

GP was not knowledgeable of planning or the suppliers; her attitude was as if her offshoring project was the only project being executed. GP was not good in research and pulling necessary information. I was informed that I was not to work on the training/offshore project, but GP was starting to suck up a lot of my time, time that I needed to launch my project.

I was receiving requests from GP that she should have already known. LL continued to request information that I had provided her several times. Rick had sabotaged me in every project that I launched to try and prove that I was incompetent. I requested a meeting with GP to find out what it is she need so that I can move forward on my project. GP and Rick was conspiring to sabotage my latest project. Once again, I had to be guarded because their final plot is now in play.

Rick sent out an e-mail that he has approved two planning requisitions internal to the organization. Only one requisition was posted and reading the description, to my surprise, it was the job that I had been performing for the past two years. I created this addition in order to help the SC be more productive.

June 25, 2009 at 4:01 PM, Rick sent this e-mail out to global planning:

Subject: Opportunity for Current Product Planning Lead

Team,

As a part of the organizational design work being done in planning, a new role will be created.

This role is described below:

Current Product Planning Lead
Act as the main point of contact for GBS planners in India to manage availability, rollovers, EOL, coordination, loss of supply, etc. Provide coaching and mentoring to India team as needed. Ensure information regarding changes in our business (e.g., strategy, initiatives, business results, etc) is well-understood and communicated to GBS team. Responsible for identifying operational risks and triggering risk mitigation plans. Ensure business objectives for inventory and availability are achieved. May include a broader role as the GBS lead for other functions in . . .

Skills required proven experience with various planning models, proven experience working with different cultures, leadership, maturity, judgment, analytical skills, ability to recognize risk, ability to train others. Must have an understanding of . . . Business and possess the ability to drive changes in strategy and tactical plans as warranted due to business conditions. Must be able to clearly and succinctly communicate status of current product operations to management.

This position will not be posted on Job Searcher, and is open to my team only. This is a critical role with significant responsibilities with a high level of visibility, and a high degree of accountability. Anyone who is qualified and interested should contact me. I intend to have a selection process, which will include an interview. I expect to make a selection by July 10.

It is possible a second position could be created for a different role, and I will communicate that information to you as it develops further. Please see me if you have any questions.

Regards,
Rick

After reading this, it blew me away. I immediately went to Rick and asked him why did he post my position. I asked him why did he pull my accomplishments and responsibilities from my evaluations and my accomplishment reports and place it as a new job.

Rick's response to me, "*Then you should apply for it.*" An interview team normally consists of three to five people; there should always be an odd person to break the locked decision. Of course, I would apply for the position. I had been working with the Asian, European, Hispanic, and Canadian team for nearly four years—training, mentoring, coaching. We were a solid team. I was the point of contact, and we did a great job for the company.

Rick mentioned there would be a panel interview, requested each applicant to submit his or her resume and time would be scheduled.

A professional panel interview consists of three or more interviewers. Each interviewer should conduct himself or herself professionally, the ability to ask proper questions and listen to the interviewee's answer. Reframe from unprofessional jesters or remarks, to act professionally and ethically at all times during the process. The interview questions should pertain to the position that is being applied for and not some other position.

As I entered the conference room, to my surprise the panel interview only consisted of Rick and GP (***red alert***). That is not a panel, and what would come next would knock your socks off.

As I set down, the first question Rick asked, "What is the religious culture of the people of India?" My response was Hindu. He went on to say, "How you know their religious background?" I responded, "I dated a gentleman from India for a short period." Then I stated, "This is an unusual question."

Religion should have nothing to do with the position; we will not be studying our beliefs so this was an inappropriate question for a manager to ask.

"Federal and state laws prohibit prospective employers from asking certain questions that are not related to the job they are hiring for. Questions should be job-related and not used to find out personal information."

In a nutshell, employers should not be asking about your race, gender, ***religion***, marital status, age, disabilities, ethnic background, country of origin, sexual preferences, or age.

Employers should not ask about any of the following because to not hire a candidate because of any one of them is discriminatory:

- Race
- Color
- Sex
- Religion
- National origin
- Birthplace

- Age
- Disability
- Marital/family status

Your Options

Answer the question.

Answer the "intent" of the question. For example, if you are asked whether you are a United States citizen (*not legal to ask*), reply that you are authorized to work in the United States, which is a question the employer can ask you and which is appropriate to answer.

Try to change the topic of conversation and avoid the question.

Refusing to answer the question might cost you the job if you are very uncomfortable with the question. However, consider whether you really want to work somewhere where you are asked questions that are not appropriate.

Before You File a Claim

Before you file a claim for discrimination, you might want to consider that most discrimination is not deliberate. In many cases, *the interviewer may simply be ignorant of the law.* Even though the interviewer may have asked an illegal question, it doesn't necessarily mean that the intent was to discriminate or that a crime has been committed.

Filing a Claim

If you believe you have been discriminated against by an employer, labor union, or employment agency when applying for a job or while on the job because of your race, color, sex, religion, national origin, age, or disability. If you believe that you have been discriminated against because of opposing a prohibited practice or participating in an equal employment opportunity matter, you may file a charge of discrimination with the *US Equal Employment Opportunity Commission* (EEOC).

Illegal Interview Questions

Questions Employers Should Not Ask
By Alison Doyle, About.com Guide

The next question asked by Rick was "Why you want this position since you are opposed to the offshoring?" GP acted as though a cobra snake climbed into her body as she was slivering her head and a roll of the eyes stated, "THAT'S WHAT I'M SAYIN," and started the rolling of the eyes.

My response, "*This is a position that I have performed for two years, I created the position, the suppliers that I manage need to know the transition is transparent, the customers need to know that there will be no interruption in their orders, and the new planners need to know the issues and be able to properly execute. The entire staff is concerned about this out sourcing because it threatens their jobs, but the company and customers should and must be the first priority.*"

The next question that came was a forecasting question; Rick asked what the days of inventory formula are. In response, "*I am no forecaster, I can tell you how we get to the required quarterly inventory to meet the company's revenue,*" as I proceeded. "*In order to meet revenue, inventory is a liability; you want just enough inventory daily to meet customer demand, as the demand is met working with the forecast it will yield the desired revenue.*"

"*We do know that the forecast is off +/—because it is working with history. Managing inventory levels will help meet the desired generated demand.*"

There were no questions asked pertaining to the position. I was able to answer the questions asked.

There were no questions in regard to how you will manage the team when there are system failures.

How would you handle mitigating circumstance with a loss of supply? These questions should have been asked for this position. Questions that are related to the position were never asked. This was the most unethical, unprofessional interview that I ever had to endure. Rick said that he and GP will make their decision in two days and get back with each of us.

After the interview, a coworker VL who had not been at HP for one year shared that he also applied. He said, "*I do not know what is going on and was not able to answer a lot of the questions; I just interviewed to see what would happen.*"

Interviewers' Bad Behavior

There is a plethora of articles providing tips for applicants in preparing for a job interview; however, there is very little material available on what makes a good *interviewer*. The result should come as no surprise that there are many bad interviewers. As a result, a poor interviewer can turn off, and possibly lose, an outstanding candidate (and potential employee). Furthermore, one can learn much about an organization's culture from the hiring process and experience.

The longer the economy struggles, the worse some employers seem to treat job seekers. And job seekers, feeling a lack of power, increasingly feel they have no choice but to put up with it.

When employers never bother to get back to interviewees with a decision after they have spent time meeting for the interview is extremely unprofessional.

Because of the economy, you will find employers who miss scheduled phone interviews with no warning or acknowledgment, often the candidate has arranged his/her schedule and waiting by the phone.

- Interviewers are often late finally meet the applicant with a weak handshake.
- An unfriendly silently leading the candidate to the conference room.
- An interviewer who is insulting, unprofessional body language, tone with a superior attitude.
- An interviewer not reading the candidates resume prior to the interview and it becomes obvious during the interview.
- Unrelated questions to the job without eye contact or rolling of the eyes.
- Interviewers who are rude, arrogant, and exude an "I hold all the cards here" attitude.

Employers who behave like this are shortsighted, unprofessional, and have no moral integrity. A good candidate would know if the employer behaves like this in an interview, this is how their future would look like if they accepted the position. This is not a company a qualified candidate would want to work no matter how bad the economy may be.

When job seekers are desperate and do not feel another opportunity will come forth soon, they accept the bad behavior of the interviewer and make the bad decision well the behavior was not too bad.

The perception is that they must tolerate this behavior in order to increase their chances to be or remain employed. If candidates are selected for a position, they typically find that the bad interviewer behavior is continued throughout the employee-employer relationship. My first interview to land the business planning position in 2006 went well overall, but Rick's attitude was always raw and off. The interview was a panel interview with five individuals, not two. In my case, I was already in the department, created the position, and continue employment under Rick would only become worse.

Rick got back to all the other candidates within the two days; I had to wait four days before he asked me to join him in the conference room.

Once we sat down, Rick stated, "I want to tell you we offered the job to VL." I responded, "OK, how did you come to that decision?" Rick stated, "He is competent, and he has a lot of experience." Then he said, "You would have gotten the job if you had answered the DOI [days of inventory question]." I stated, "This is what I said to you in the interview, '*I am no forecaster. I can tell you how we get to the required quarterly inventory to meet the company's revenue, as I proceeded. In order to meet revenue, inventory is a liability, you want just enough inventory daily to meet customer demand, as the demand is met working with the forecast it will yield the desired revenue.*'"

Rick responded, "If you had said that in the interview, the job would have been yours." I responded, "That is exactly what I said."

As the conversation continued, Rick said, "There may be another position coming up that you can apply." Then Rick said, "*We have had a pretty stormy relationship, you reported me to HR for your salary, you reported me to Mark because of your evaluation, you fail to realize I am the manager not Mark.*" I stated, "*Mark has been my mentor, I continued to speak with him to know how to get along with you.*" I asked Rick, "Why did the interview panel consist of two people, and why did he allow GP to roll her eyes at me and speak to me with such a demean attitude?" Rick responded, "I cannot make people like you, and if she wants to roll her eyes, I cannot stop her."

I reminded Rick that he said this type of behavior will not be tolerated, and why is it allowed to be practiced by GP; he recanted and said he would speak with her and get back to me on Monday. I do not understand how I created a position and have been very successful only to have the position given to someone else. Rick stated, "You need to train VL," and then he said, "your planning will not go away immediately, issues need to be cleared up before going to VL." Then he stated, "If Ben is not successful in the training of the India team, it will be his job."

I asked, "How is that fair since it is my suppliers that you are asking him to train the team on, he do not know what is going on with my suppliers." Rick suggested, "Training is up to Ben, if he wants you on the team, that is up to him, but he better be successful."

Now it is Wednesday. I shared Rick's information with Ben. Ben's response was "Yes, he said the same to me." This company and organization is a cesspool, and the employees have folded into it like a blanket. All employees are sharing cubes, which is office space, two to a cube like cattle in a stock farm. Ben slides into the aisle and calls me by my first initial. He said, "I have an idea, I would like you to train the India team on your suppliers, you have all the knowledge, and I think that would be best."

Immediately, GP shoved her chair into the cubical wall and marched over to Ben and my section. As she spoke to Ben in an angry tone, she proceeded, "I do not want that women to have anything to do with training the India team," pointing her finger at me, then she abruptly told Ben come with me. As they exited the area, about ten minutes later Ben came back to his desk extremely upset, then I saw GP ask Rick to take a walk with her. Ben was upset. I walked over to Ben and said, "I do not want to put any pressure on you." SL came over to the area, and I stated, "I just want what is best for you. I did not want Rick to follow through on his threat, the offer to help you was on the table." SL said, "Just *say no* Ben, just say no."

LL stood up and injected herself into the conversation as she often did. I informed her that she was not knowledgeable in regard to the chain of events; she was not in the area. LL requested, "Well, train me and I will take it to the team." In response, I cannot, and I do not want anyone to say that I tried to sabotage the training.

I notified the team that I was leaving on a retreat and have a good weekend. I returned to work the following Monday. Rick called me on the phone and asked me to join him in the conference room.

I had no clue what he wanted. I walked in the room, and he stated I have HR on the phone. I asked what this is about, and he stated, "I am placing you on probation for misconduct." I stood up and said, "I would like Mark in here." Rick rose up, slammed his hand on the table, said, "Shut up, and sit down, this is my meeting. I told you if you upset your coworkers, I will escort you out of here."

Once again, as comely as I could, I asked what this is about; he said you could be heard screaming over the building at Ben about the training. I stated comely that never happened. He went on to say Ben came to me very upset and said you screamed at him. Of course, I defended myself and said, "No, GP yelled at him and then took him away. After she returned, she took you away." GP is the only one that was acting unprofessional on Wednesday.

After leaving the conference room, I spoke with Mark; as he pretended he had no clue about what was going on when indeed he was in the middle of it. In your working situation, realize you cannot always trust what your manager communicates to you. This practice is often done when they think the employee may go postal, they often play good manager bad manager to find out what you are thinking and what you plan on doing.

I lodged a complaint with HR after speaking with the VP of our organization.

TA of HR requested time to investigate. I mentioned that I was going to file a complaint with EEOC. TA requested that this decision be delayed in filing with EEOC and give her a chance to conduct an investigation.

Remember this, *HR can never request an employee to delay exercising his/her rights to file with EEOC. Be aware, when that request is made, termination is imminent.* I asked for the rest of the day off, went to the EEOC, and filed a complaint. Never go to EEOC empty handed, always have proof of your complaint to be a part of the record. Even though EEOC may be backed up due to lack of staff, it is easier for EEOC to assess your problem with all the information than with less. I took all the necessary proof with me, Rick's treatment, his e-mails, the fabricated probation, and the fact that his punishment was unjust.

After filing with EEOC, the retaliation from Rick became very evident. The first thing Rick did was to remove all my responsibilities. I was in the midst of investigating why my supplier produced $1.5 million of a product that would no longer be needed. The trigger went out a year prior, knowing that the product was being removed; Rick contacted the supplier that I managed and signed a contract to produce a massive amount inventory.

Can you see what length this man went to, and note the time, it was one year prior. Rick had communicated to Mark that the trigger was not sent. Rick was not approved to sign contracts for this dollar amount. I do believe his approval amount was $25,000. Once the proof was produced that the trigger went out, the cover-up started.

In speaking with Mark, his response was "Let's see where the breakdown was, let's not lay blame, let's wait, and see what the outcome would be."

I later understood that Rick's hatred for me was because of his own inadequacies. Mark made a great mistake placing Rick in the position of planning supervisor. Rick was not strong in his knowledge of supply chain—how dare an African American female know more than a middle-age racist white man. Every sabotage, every unfair project, the increase workload, Rick was extremely disappointed that an African American female was intelligent enough to be successful over all the pitfalls that he put in place.

I happened to be under the wrong manager at the wrong time. It could have been any African American that worked for Rick, his hatred for the nationality that I am proud to be born into. I understand that a person like Rick lacks intelligence and experiences his/her own inferiority. Rick is the type of person that most likely was bullied as a child, possibly by African Americans, people of color, or had parents that were very racist and raised, molded, and developed a person that would promote this hatred.

Mark on the other hand portrayed the personality of a coward. He throws a rock and then hide his hand so know one would know that he privately attacked you.

A company that keeps these types of people in management is not a company that an ethical person would want to work under or be associated. The company has now fired its third CEO; this signal of instability has been repeated over and over and over again.

CHAPTER

5

The Agreement

Mark, Rick, and TA of HR knew the complaint that was made about Rick was serious, and I was not backing off it. They have now been notified by EEOC that a complaint has been made and an investigation would take place. TA knew that she did not properly investigate the concerns that I lodge to her, a confidential conversation that was made with her was broken. TA called Rick and Mark and shared everything that was discussed. In addition, the three of them decided to try to convince me they have my best interest in mind.

Mark was at fault for not taking action after he failed to report to HR that there was a complaint of racial discrimination. Mark also covered up Rick's signing of a $1.5 million contract with a supplier that he had no authorization to sign. In addition, Rick and Mark had been fudging the numbers reported regarding the revenue reports on inventory. Once I would not play ball and become the fall guy, it was their plan to remove me and once removed to say I did not follow through on sending out the trigger.

A meeting was set up, Rick, Mark, TA on conference and myself. In this meeting, the three of them tried to persuade me in dropping my lawsuit and accept a mutual separation agreement, which would give me more than I would get by merely being laid off. TA not realizing that I had sixteen years of HR, she fabricated what the mutual separation agreement was about. I did tape this meeting as well as other meetings with Rick and Mark

My friend at that time, SL, strongly encouraged me to tape the conversations due to Rick's being a habitual liar. The meeting went for about one hour; I listened to everything they had to say, their lies, their desperation, as well as Mark trying to play the devil's advocate.

Once the meeting was over, Mark suggested that I go on medical leave to collect my thoughts, get my health in order, and let him know what I decide to do. Mark was trying to promote goodwill so that I would drop my lawsuit. I took the time to relax and try to recover; I also took the time to build my case against this unethical company and these two managers. I mentioned earlier that when employees are treated as I would often go postal. I understand why people would retaliate against their employers. People like Mark and Rick make the decision easy for people to make the decision to go postal, but when a person come to the decision to go in the work place and shoot their manager, it makes them as indecent as the managers they shot.

I cannot stress this enough, even though it seems like unethical people like Rick and Mark will get away with treating people unfair. Trust me, they will only bask in their glory for a short season. When they think they have gotten away with their scheming, plotting, setting up, lying, etc., then they will fall into their own trap.

I said that to say this, do not use your energy, decency, thoughts, or actions on retaliating against bad managers because God will have the final say and you may be blessed to see it. Use the law to send the message to let these companies know that it is not OK to treat people in an unethical way. As I returned at the beginning of 2010 from medical leave, I arrived back into a climate of hostility. Once you decide to file against your company with EEOC, know that life will be very uncomfortable. An ignorant manager will retaliate and not adhere to the employment law or any other law this was Rick and Mark.

Mark spoke with me and stated, "*You need to speak with Rick and find out your next position,*" and even though Mark knew that he and Rick had already asked HR to slate me for early retirement. I stated, "I know Rick's desire is to terminate." Mark denied that was the case. I set up a meeting with Rick in an open setting. Rick tried to persuade me into going into a conference room, and I refused.

I knew if we had the meeting would have been volatile, I would not have tolerated another episode of yelling, finger pointing, or demeaning criticism from Rick again. I would have reacted in a volatile way and knowing that I requested an open setting.

Rick let me know that my job had been transferred to India and that I would not have the opportunity to apply for any positions within the company. He gave me paperwork supporting his statement. Once I received the paperwork, I notified Rick that I would be submitting this paperwork to EEOC; no employment action was to be taken until the investigation was concluded.

At that point, Rick and Mark wanted the paperwork back and stated, "You are not being fired." Mark stated, "You are being retired so that you can get your health together." I left, went to EEOC, and submitted the latest paperwork. EEOC could not believe that the manager would be so stupid to take such actions.

At this point, I no longer wanted to be a part of such a company. I watched how people of color were being treated. A few of my friends had to apply and interview for positions that they had worked in for a long period. This is the face of racism; this is the new slavery in corporate America.

Chapter

6

Seeking an Attorney

Good employment attorneys are very difficult to find. Not many are confident in going up against large notable companies. Those that are confident may have so many clients that they cannot give your case the attention that is needed. Remember, you are interviewing the attorney, do your research, ask around. Google is a wonderful tool to research as well as locating a great attorney.

In interviewing attorneys, make sure the attorney will receive payment only if they win the case. If the attorney requests that you pay a percentage prior to him taking the case, continue to look. You will have to pay a consultation fee with most attorneys. When you go into the office, pay attention how well the attorney listens to you. Note how many times they allow disruptions while consulting with you. An attorney that is a stickler in time that if you are thirty minutes over and he charges you, which is not the attorney for you. Disruptions eat away at time you have paid for, so if you go over, you have already paid for the time.

When the attorney wants to continue to tell you about other cases instead of talking about what he or she would do with your case, redirect the attorney's attention back to the case at hand.

You often hear attorneys are in it for the money. This is true—everyone wants to get paid. An attorney that listens, believes in your case, and will work hard for you is worth their weight in gold. An attorney that mediates more than he/she goes to court may or may not be the attorney you want to represent you.

Make sure that you do not fabricate any portion of your complaint. Prior to leaving your company, those that state they will be a witness for you, have them to write and sign a statement supporting your complaint. Witnesses often retract their statements when it is time for deposition.

Once you retain an attorney, make the agreement that he/she will interview your witnesses right away. When the attorney does not speak to the witnesses and allows a time lapse, the witnesses will lose their boldness and side with the company.

Management always persuades witnesses to support the company by giving them large salary increases, bonuses, and yes, even promises for long employment if they support the company and not support their friend that is suing the company. Know that your witnesses will turn on you for the sake of the company. That is why it is important to secure statements prior to your exit.

Always remember you experienced the nightmare that brought you to this point. As your attorney tries to tell you how your employer will behave, remember your attorney only knows them through your experience, not his/hers, insist that he/she listen to you and not develop his/her own story.

Again, Google is a wonderful tool to find an employment law attorney. If one says they cannot take your case due to their workload, continue to research, and seek—you will find one.

Attorneys know that companies are using unethical practices to remove employees in the hope that these employees will not bother following up with a lawsuit. If the company offers a severance and convinces the employee that this is the better choice, file the lawsuit. You will receive more in retribution than you will if you accepted the severance. With severance, you will pay 48 percent in taxes and walk away with nothing.

You will have to pay your attorney up front for administration cost, court fees, and deposition fee, which may be around $5,000 to $7,000. It is not your attorney's responsibility to pay this for you. Your attorney is not paying you to take your case. You are paying him/her. Everyone wants to get paid; you will recover much, much more in your lawsuit. Find out how many times the attorney has appeared before a judge. If you mediate and do not go to court, then there is no record that the company was sued. You want to persuade your attorney to go to court and not settle. The mediator is not on your side. The mediator is there for one reason and that is to settle the case. Often times the attorney will lowball you, stick to what you know you deserve.

Once you have retained an attorney, it may take up to a year before you have your deposition. The company's attorney will try and destroy your character; she/he will construct an image that you are crazy, unsuccessful, unqualified, difficult to work with, a liar, etc.

She/he has been paid to be ruthless; they will try every trick in the book to get the case thrown out of court. He/she will embellish the truth; in other words, they will build a case of lies against you, hope that your attorney is adequate, and respond strongly.

The manager will be in the deposition. He/she will try to intimidate you. Just remember, this is your day to tell what happened. This is your voice that will be heard, continue to be polite because the defending attorney will not be polite.

As your witnesses come through, you will be able to witness their depositions as well as your managers. Funny thing, managers will lie unto their graves. They will not tell the truth to save their own lives. Depending on how threatened the defending attorney feels, he/she will push for mediation because they will know if the judge refuses to hear the case. Out of court, they stand a strong chance of losing the case. When you go to a mediator, realize he/she receives payment regardless if you settle or not. The mediator does not care how much you receive; he/she plays both ends against the middle and convince your attorney to follow his lead.

Big companies do not want to go to court, especially when they know they are wrong. Often they will push for a settlement, hold out, and get what you deserve. Do not allow your attorney to lowball you. Make your attorney listen to you. Attorneys and mediators embellish their stories they tell you about past cases, they tell you some of the truth and a lot of untruth to get you to think they have your best interest in mind.

Pay attention to the agreement that you sign with your attorney. Most will say 40 percent if they win, and often they will slip in a clause 45 percent pretrial. If they do not go to trial, they still charge you a pretrial percentage if they settle close to your trial date, which is not quite fair.

If you choose to settle, do not sign the agreement until you have read line by line, page by page. Often, companies will throw clauses that will rob you of your settlement, and attorneys often do not follow through because it does not affect their 40-45 percent. You can still walk away with almost nothing if you do not read the entire agreement.

If there has been physical harm, for instance health issues from stress that you have incurred medical problems have that considered if you settle. The government now tax lawsuits. You want your retribution to be 80 percent bodily harm and 20 percent severance. The severance will be taxed 45-50 percent. Do not sign the settlement unless the defending attorney and company agree to these terms.

Anytime you have to file a lawsuit nobody really wins. The company has spent thousands of dollars to fight you and still have to pay you. You have just endured a few years of injustice, but now you are able to move on.

I encourage you to write your story, for every person that has fallen prey to an employment situation that a lawsuit had to be filed, tell your story.

The more of us that dare to share our experience, the more people we can help, the more companies will think twice before they promote unethical behavior amongst their managers, the more CEOs will read our stories and try to form a better company that promote equality.

My town is San Diego. Your place may be Germany, Japan, New York, Georgia, Canada, Oklahoma, Texas, Pennsylvania, Arizona, etc. No matter where the companies that violate your employment rights are located, just know it is against the law to practice any of the offenses listed below.

My attorney David Miller said, "Your employment rights are the scales of justice weighed against you at work."

- Wrongful termination
- Retaliation
- Pay problems

- Harassment
- Discrimination
- Unfair discipline

These actions are against the law. If you feel you have been treated unfairly, do not go "postal," retain a lawyer.

I really hope that sharing my story will help those of you that are going through what I have experienced. If your employer is practicing any of the above behavior, do not take a severance, mutual separation agreement, or walk off the job. Retain an employment attorney and "FIGHT FOR YOUR RIGHTS."

Tell your story, write your book, and share your legal situation, share advice by paying it forward. If these companies provide products to the public, encourage your friends and family members not to support them—do not purchase their goods. Every time we purchase products these companies provide, we are supporting the very behavior that we are fighting. We are keeping these people employed; there are several ways to fight companies fraught with employment violations:

1. File with EEOC
2. Retain an attorney
3. Do not purchase their products
4. Communicate this behavior to your friends and family
5. Encourage those you know not to apply for positions at these companies

This is the better way to fight. Good luck in your pursuit for justice.

NOTES:

Attorney's phone numbers:

_____

_____

_____

_____

_____

What laws have my managers broken: (Dates)

_____

_____

_____

_____

Witness written and signed statements:

_____

_____

_____

_____

_____

_____

Supporting e-mails:

_____

_____

_____

_____

_____